WAKENING BETWEEN WORLDS

Wakening

Between Worlds

POEMS

Xiaoly Li

SERVING HOUSE BOOKS

Wakening Between Worlds
Copyright © 2026 Xiaoly Li
First Edition

All rights reserved. No part of this book may be reproduced or transmitted in any form or by any means, electronic, digital, or mechanical, including photocopy, audio recording, or any information storage and retrieval system, without prior permission from the publisher or author (except by reviewers who may quote brief passages). No part of this book may be used or reproduced in any manner for the purpose of training artificial intelligence technologies or systems. Any references to historical events, real people, or real places are used fictitiously in this work of fiction.

Cover art: Xiaoly Li
Art on dedication page: Huang Zhongqi

Cover design by Jacob Arms
Paperback ISBN: 9781947175822

Published by Serving House Books
Lawrence Landing Company
Raleigh, North Carolina 27609
United States of America
www.servinghousebooks.com

Serving House Books is a proud member of

Independent Book Publishers Association
 and
Community of Literary Magazines and Presses

ADVANCE PRAISE

Xiaoly Li's latest collection *Wakening Between Worlds* is a true discovery of identity. These poems narrate the poet's heritage through magic and myth. It is in the unique ecological moments like the first time at the ocean where "each trace of us erased by waves" is another way the poet signifies bravery. Through persona, ars poetica, or just Li's nuanced language, she brings us with her— to beauty, to pain where "every step a wound" breaks us as readers. Though, no matter where she takes us, we end each poem transcended.

—Alexis Ivy, author of *Taking the Homeless Census*

Li's exquisite *Waking Between Worlds* chronicles a life of regime change, childhood deprivation, forced familial separation, and immigration, and never refuses the comfort of the flora and fauna of the earth or of remembered and present beauty. Li's inner compass is *the love that holds us, living or dead,* and her poems will replenish any reader again and again.

—Marcela Sulak, author of *The Fault* and the National Jewish Book Award Finalist, *City of Skypapers*

Wakening Between Worlds is the bravest of books. Xiaoly Li, born and raised in China, writes beautifully in a language and a sensibility not hers from birth. Her family history and the revolution underline the book, told with delicacy and without blame, the privation of her early years sleeping in a pigsty, scarcity of food they shared with the starving, even bean-cakes meant for pigs. We get palpable details, a bed the family used as a ping-pong table, street-vendors hawking red hawthorne ices in their Beijing neighborhood. The ancient poets visit her, inform her voice. Past and present intertwine throughout. At times she calls on forms: haiku, cinquain, shadorma. She tells us again and again of her awe of the natural world, observing the murder of one species by another, she recognizes we are all predators. Sometimes she imagines herself a bird, longing to fly, to escape the confines of her life. With the baby daughter she was forced to leave in China for several years, now an adult in the US, she is tender and tentative, careful not to burden her with love. And slowly her daughter returns to her. In the end, Xiaoly Li reclaims herself: *Here I am/* O my little girl, my little self.

—Margot Wizansky,
 author of *Random Music in a Small Galaxy*

The first time I read *Wakening Between Worlds* I sat with each poem, let it settle in me; I wanted to feel them, one at a time, before I thought them, something immediately apparent in the author's approach, too. 'I wrote my first poem / the first time I saw the ocean, ' writes Xiaoly Li, and thus does an intricate, dewed, singularly tender history begin. Through the turning of the natural world, this poet carefully, intentionally, walks us through a life—one with a questioning, persistent, openly admiring viewpoint that invites, via meditative offering, entry to her world.

Through single-stroke nature studies and a pantheon of intimate personae, this work reveals the author's graceful connections between history and our own sense of self that we carry forward from turbulence and the human tendency to harm. 'But what do I know of God's beauty? Humans / prey on each other, and on many others, as well' she writes. The Chinese diaspora is glorious in these pages. History and personae here vibrate with knowing, with understanding. But so too does the great love of a writer longing for a gentler way of being in the world, for a softer humanity. And maybe it's out of our reach, 'Why can't I become who I aspire to be? 'she asks. In these poems Xiaoly Li answers that question, and in so doing, moves past it, standing bare under 'ever-changing clouds.'"

>—Tennison Black, author of *Survival Strategies*, winner of the National Poetry Series 2022, and the AZ Book Award in poetry, 2024

CONTENTS

ONE

In the Spring of My Youth 1
Under the Veil of Spring 2
Your Breath Mingles with Theirs 3
What I Once Called Home 4
Meeting the Great Ancients 5
My Generation 6
After the Dragon Boat Festival 7
Horn Pond in May 8
In Our Cypress 9
Dichotomy 10
The Killdeer 11
Yeye and Me 12
Grains of Sand—Collection of Haiku 13
Yun Er, Could Child, My Betta Fish 14
Echoes of the Eclipse 15
In New York City 16
Juliets 17
Two Twelve-Spotted Skimmer 18

TWO

Firefly 21
I See No Animals in the Clouds 22
On Marriage 23
Legacy in Loess 24
To the People, Food is the Sky 25
Between the Sun and Moon 27
A Sheet of Blank Paper 29
When I'm walking backwards 30

Island of Cows—São Miguel, Azores 31
Ocean Songs 32
Moonlight Walk.. 34
A Journey Toward the Ocean 35
When Dragons Come 36
In the Night 37
Cloud Rose... 38

THREE

Under the Autumn High Sky 41
The Missing River 42
Unsung, Five Cinquains 43
Shuffling Through Old Photographs.......................... 44
My Popo Talks to the Air... 45
The Weight of Time... 46
Autumn Peach 47
The Wind of Emptiness... 48
Walking the DogBar Breakwater at 49
My New Festivals 50
Andrew Jackson's Hermitage in 51
Unsettled 52
Fixed 53
Horizons 54
Moon Goddess Chang'e Gazing 55
Trace 56
A Collection of Shadorma 57
Diana and the Archer 58
Echoes of Birds... 59
Great Meadows in the Autumn 60

FOUR

Fresh Winter 63
Horn Pond Haikus 64
Heavenly Eyes 66
Su-Mei from Su-Zhou, China 68
Swallow Brand 69
In a Brutal Winter 70
In the Great Darkness 71
The Mystical Blue Rabbit Stamp 72
New Year 73
Sighting a Snowy Owl 74
This Body is Not Mine 75
Mind Body Duet 76
When the Body Becomes Replaceable Parts 78
Winter in the Great Meadows 79
The Great Migration 80
Lotus Pond 81
Wakening Between Worlds 82
Acknowledgments   85

To my husband and my daughter, my first readers,
and to my parents.

The moon falls   crows cry   frost fills the sky,
river maples   fishing light   upon worried sleep.
Outside Gusu city lies Hanshan temple,
a midnight bell chimes to the traveller boat.

—from "Night Mooring by Maple Bridge" by Zhang Ji
(ca. 712-715 to 779)

Translated by Xiaoly Li

ONE

Spring of My Youth

I wrote my first poem
the first time I saw the ocean,
my heart thumped.
You and I lay on the beach,
until dusk when a guard
asked us to leave.

I remember you sang
Carry away a light
from the boat. Moor love
at the maple bridge. We walked
along the shoreline, each trace
of us erased by waves.

When my days feel blue,
I return to the ocean where
the shore stares at each
coming and going
and its roaring floods my ears
and settles my heart.

Under the Veil of Spring

Pine seedlings take root in granite cracks,
when spring frost withers peaches' bloom.

The sudden cold snuffs peaches' flowering,
while a heron feasts on tender cygnets.

The poised heron claims cygnets' lives. Aching
like your first kiss lost in the empty breeze.

Your first kiss fades in the empty breeze.
The wind caresses stones with unfurled words.

Etched on stones, tales of unfurled words,
where primal urges surge, untamed, unknown.

As primal urges rage, blood spills and stains,
Salmon fights fiercely under the eagles' dive.

Salmon thrashes free from the eagle's clasp,
Pine seedlings sprout up from granite cracks.

Your Breath Mingles with Theirs

Go to the garden.
Kiss green bean seeds
before tucking them into soil.
Sing to puffballs of chives.
Pray the tomatoes are bountiful.
Hum to the cucumbers,
talk to them, touch them.

Go to a summit along the Atlantic Flyway.
Search for the migrating birds,
the red-tailed hawk,
its effortless soaring.
I whistle back to the long-winged harrier,
bless the peregrine falcon
before it vanishes south.

I listen to nature's whispers,
and speak with a tender voice,
there will be listeners.

What I Once Called Home

What can time hold? Not the place where we lived in the 1980s, Shanmen Hu Tong, named in the year the imperial dynasty ended. Not a single trace of my Hu Tong—mazes of narrow lanes, our two-room house, one courtyard, one water faucet under a big open sky, shared by three families, a wooden bed we used as a ping pong table lying on top of four chairs in the thick, warm air. Look now at those glassy buildings in the heart of Beijing. Bulky high rises push the sky farther away.

What can satisfy the insatiable taste buds? Not the abundant restaurants— Peking Duck, Palace food, Italian Pizza, Japanese sushi… Ringing in my ears. I miss the vendor's callings echoed in the Hu Tong, *Ice-sugar gourds!* The tower of red hawthorns on each bamboo stick, covered in ice-sugar, glossy, sweet and sour.

What can history recover? The White Pagoda Temple near my Hu Tong. We walk in the flurry of downy catkins—ancient secrets uncovered— a mantra written in Emperor Qianlong's own hand, a carving of Guanyin made from yellow sandalwood. Not the walnut tree towering next to our window—we twisted stems and coaxed nuts down with a bamboo hook in the crispy air. Their green shells blackened my hands and took days to wash away.

Meeting the Great Ancients

In a mountain of plum trees, I meet Lu You,
the poet of the defeated Song Dynasty.
He stops beside every tree, whether blossoming or
flowers falling. He strides like a soldier brandishing a
sword, too great to follow. I stop on the hilltop and aim
my camera toward him. His figure appears everywhere,
yet he is elusive. The fragrance endures.

At the sea, I find Li Shangyin under a huge late Tang
Dynasty moon beaming a thousand rays kissing each
wave. He stands still, facing the moon. I walk over
quietly and sit on a rock. Turning to me, his eyes flash a
starry night sky like warm tears. I wait for him to tell
passing stories.

I wait until after Li Bai, poet of Tang Dynasty, finishes
three jugfuls of wine, raises his head, sighs, holds the
cup toward the sky, laughing. He invites the moon and
his shadow to join him in dance. His voice enchants;
I dance with him in the garden around orchids through
the pines.

My Generation

I was born after my parents' return from the forgotten war, when mothers with many children were hailed as heroes.

I survived on wild vegetables picked with Nainai, my grandma. Famine persisted for years.

We went to school but did not study in the Cultural Revolution. We roamed streets, shouting his slogans—
Revolution is not a crime, rebellion is justified!

In our late teens, we toiled in the countryside,
our hands calloused, feet soiled,
in fields and pigsties.

Love became taboo in our youth. Girls and boys were segregated. One girl had a forbidden boyfriend. We called her a caterpillar.

In our maturity, the marriage age was defined, the one child policy decreed. Like ancient women's feet, our every step a wound.

After the Dragon Boat Festival

A dandelion claws the lawn like a dragon
breathing its wild yellow flower.

One, two, three... a blanket of them, we dig them out
and throw them into the waste bin.

Now the turf expands a uniform green,
the air scented with cut-grass.

Seeds already parachute on the breeze
into forgotten corners like erased history

over our rivers where Wu Zixu, Qu Yuan,
wronged by the emperors, drowned

themselves. Their spirit survives the way
dandelions keep coming,

sprouting like shadows of dragons, where
poppies have fallen, becoming scarlet dust.

Horn Pond in May

        Late, yet arrives warm light. With her red beak
and a wiggle of her white body, the swan stirs the mud
for eight cygnets to feed.

Today, only three swanlings remain. I curse the
snapping turtle, its wrinkled, fierce face
bubbling on the water's surface.

But what do I know of God's beauty? Humans
prey on each other, on many others, as well.

        On this crowded dam the cannons of cameras
aim at stocky night herons,

whose red eyes stare into the water.
We catch them striking, seizing fish.

Wa! Beautiful! We disregard
the last twists of the fish.

        On the cherry tree beside the pond,
four hatchlings burst from robin blue, open

their mouths as I pass. Now only the nest
remains, woven with dry yellow hay,
sea blue plastic mesh, white tissue,
wafting in the wind,
like my frozen smile.

In Our Cypress

In front of our house, the hatchling stands all day, not moving anywhere since morning. Black and white feathers dazzle & her eyes mirror the neighbor's house & the sky. She looks at me with no fear.

She grew out of the last blue egg, near naked. When her eyes opened later, she knew I wasn't her mother. She appears so comely now, her feathers thick yet short.

By evening, the tree stands empty of her—
in the grass, blood on her de-feathered neck,
a hole in her chest,
a half-bitten leg beside the tree.

Next day I seen the bird's mother and find her in our rock garden gathering up straw again...

Dichotomy

The snake's scales gleam yellow and black.
He's engulfing the bulgy eyed frog,
whose throat and chest heave raw.

The frog contracts with each gulp, gasping
for air. My heart shamed, I remember night-
caught frogs cooked delicious and spicy by my
kindergarten teachers.

My sympathy is with the frog now. His croak is music.
His song fills twilight, a symphony
of double bass in the nearby pond.

I'm not keen on the snake, but I have saved
his molted skin, *dragon's rope*, a treasure
in Chinese medicine, in my jewelry box.

With their serpentine bodies, Nüwa
the mother Goddess, and Fuxi the Sage
entwined, they created our ancestors.

The frog is less visible now from the stretch
of the snake's mouth. The snake slithers
back to the hole in the granite wall.

The wisest tactic on the battlefield
from the ancient *Thirty-Six Stratagems*, is to retreat. I
can no longer watch.

The Killdeer

I walk alongside the wetlands where reeds glisten in the sun. I hear chirping. A killdeer blocks my path and flaps her wings, with a white belly, brown back, and black stripes on her neck. She must be wounded. I kneel down to check.

But she screeches, steps closer, her wings tremble in a frenzy, and her tail fans out, radiating a golden shine. She looks large to me now and screams me away from her circle of seven stones, each as big as herself.

In the middle, three bare eggs, blotched chocolate. So, I pass gently around her nest. She embraces the eggs with open wings.

Yeye and Me

Yeye, my grandfather takes me for walks.
He says words that are hard for me
such as *Philosophy* and *Art*.
So I name him Arty. As he sits
to smoke, I sniff around,
pick hawthorn leaves
to ease my stomach and seek
smooth trunks of tall sycamore trees,
to leave my mark.
After a cigarette, Arty sings
Peking Opera. When I mimic the tune
he laughs to tears.
A specialty between us.

Sometimes we won't be home until
crickets chirp under the fading sun.
Mom often gives me a whole egg:
You keep Grandpa healthy.

They shout at each other
once in a while, faces red.
You are my forever love,
he says to me.

*I'll make a contract
with you for the next life*,
he extends his hand
with the blue veins on it,
I give him my paw.

Grains of Sand—Collection of Haiku

Lotus Effect

Lotus leaf repels,
un-cling rain's teardrop to dance.
Nature's secret spell.

Reborn

Bearing worry's weight,
like the child she holds within,
She births it in words.

Mirrors of LIGO

The invisible
light year's whisper, gravity,
dwarfed by endlessness.

Yun Er, Cloud Child, My Betta Fish

I long for you,
a shooting star, a kiss,
too brief to catch.

You are leaving,
taking a cloud away,
betta blue.

You have been hiding
under the arrowhead plant,
and chosen to stray.

You used to swim toward me,
whenever I approached.

I leaned my hand on your brandy bowl,
kiss me, kiss me, I said.

You chased my fingers,
gazed at and grazed each one
a light, flying touch.

Echoes of the Eclipse

I craft an eclipse camera with a solar lens,
chasing the moon—the celestial dog—
as it swallows the sun's golden apple.

The sun's warmth fades, my dog barks.
Darkness converges with light.
A black hole spits out a corona blaze.

Some fear an apocalypse nears.
Some bathe and seek forgiveness.
Others vow and make love
beneath the astral ring.

I feel a chill and tiny as birds fall silent.
The small moon can shield the mighty sun
and umbrella the earth when three align.

So too, can our imagination reach the stars.

Yet the celestial dog must release
what it swallowed.
And so I decide to let you live—

in the light,
in the mystery of shadow.

The sun and moon journey on as before,
leaving me spinning with the earth.

In New York City

This time, something fresh simmers in my daughter's
place. For the first time she and her partner invite us
to stay with them—

Compact rooms hold a glass coffee table,
a moveable spice cart, and a spinning bike.
She flings open the windows. The scent of rooftop
redbuds rushes in. My daughter bicycles, lifts weights,
and unwinds with yoga. My heart unwinds from
fretting about their swift-paced life. For the first time,
she throws a bash for my birthday, something new
about her. She holds my book of poems.

Out of the window, I see glass buildings mirroring each
other, the varied forms, like Picasso's paintings. As she
and I mirror each other. Something shifts between us.
She once felt like a stranger. Did my affection burden
her? They cook frozen broccoli with Sichuan pepper,
green beans, and quinoa. I have to admit it looks
verdant and tastes good, even though it isn't fresh.

I don't mind leaving this city, its thinly stretched sky,
and its forest of towering buildings, back to my quiet
countryside with an unobstructed sky, knowing she has
wings, untethered from the kite string in my hand.

Juliets

One buries its head under its wing
as the other combs through the feathers
then the first does the combing.

Near the pond they take turns
warming their several eggs.
Year after year, they try
to hatch chicks in vain.

They were named Romeo and Juliet — the traditional
name for Boston Public Garden's swan pair.

In the year gay marriage was legalized
people learned they were Juliet & Juliet.

She and she, dressed in pure white
calmly sit, one on the nest, one beside her.

Two Twelve-Spotted Skimmer Dragonflies
—a Lai poem

Atop bamboo stick
Where yam vines twine thick
You pose
One leaves in a flick
Love you, words I speak
So close
I tiptoe—we click
You land—my hand pink
Wild rose

TWO

Firefly

Haze
sinks into dusk
upon the Blue Ridge.

Little disco stars
flit and hover

like a thousand
silver bells,
flashing on the trees,

chattering
one melody
like Christmas chorus.

I hold
sweet cold lightning
in my hands,

releasing—
my heart breaks
into countless stars.

I See No Animals in the Clouds

Look, a frog.
No, it's a rabbit.
Two little girls, across our street
wearing the identical pink dresses
point at the sky.

I only glance at the sky
when sapphire blue
is too vivid to miss
& the sun is dazzling.
The clouds line up
with the contrail of a jet.

I used to lie down in the grass
stare at the sky.
A horse drifted by, and turned
into a phoenix.
I left open the book, *Song of Youth*,
on the bamboo mat where grasshoppers
skipped my touch.

I think of Stephen Hawking watching clouds
without moving even his eyes,
speaking by slight twitches in his cheek,
his mind roaming the cosmos.

On Marriage

> *...first...there were only Nüwa and her brother, in Kunlun... making a prayer: If Heaven sends us as husband and wife, let smoke gather; if not, let smoke disperse.*
>
> — Li Rong, Zuyizhi, Tang Dynasty

Two stars collide into one life
around Webb's pond.
Two trees join rings,
becoming one.

Two walk. They see
one fish curving, rotating, dancing.
Look again, it is two fish swimming as one—
head to head or head to tail.

How long can two stay close?
One lifts, like a kite
into the distance.
The other pulls
& anchors to the earth,

the way oppressive heat
dries the pond & dispirits trees.
Smoke appears.
Will it gather or disperse?

Legacy in Loess

What could I hear from this ancient land,
from tales of women's trials?

Before women had to struggle to control their wombs,
in the primal days, Goddess Nüwa was alone.
She created humans from loess, the yellow mud.

Before women rose to serve in all roles,
Mulan of the Northern Wei Dynasty disguised
as a man, galloped and battled in place of her father.

Before women yearned to govern,
Empress Wu Zetian of the Tang Dynasty
led the country for forty years.

Later in the Song dynasty,
in agony women still bound their feet, praised
as three-inch golden lotus.

Time is not an arrow but a spiral.
I hear echoes of women from thousands of years ago—
waning, waxing, wilting, waking.

To the People, Food is the Sky

— Ban Gu, Eastern Han Dynasty

Our sky was limited when I was young, quota stamps for grain, for cooking oil, for meat, eggs, cloth, for a bicycle. I couldn't wait for my birthday to get a 10¢ ice cream bar instead of a 5¢ popsicle.

I remember the first time Father was mad at me because I dropped a few grains of rice into the table's crevice and refused to eat them. He pushed me, and I stumbled onto the table and chipped a tooth.

Our appetites could devour the sky, but we ate fresh produce from farms, ripe, untainted—tomatoes, Napa cabbages, daikons…Nothing was tastier than the memories of free-range chicken—Father got the head; Mother, wings; me, the feet, chewy, long-lasting.

We hosted a few parties with food. Our neighbor said, *It's not about food but friendship*. Each time we invited her, she took heartburn medicine just before eating our homemade dumplings. *I'll make a monument for the one who invented dumplings,* she said.

My Popo ate a bowl of chicken soup right before leaving for heaven so she would not be a Starving Ghost; her children & grandchildren would not be hungry in life. Yet when I dream about eating, I aways lose my turn.

Today, the sky has expanded to a bounty of offerings. My desire is limited by my body's needs. I must measure every meal—2/3 cup of rice, vegetables, fruit, and two fingers of protein.

My eyes still aim for more, only my eyes.

Between the Sun and Moon

The sun starts to soften its rays. You come, bald eagle,
    reclaiming a half-moon
      behind your thousand-feathered wings. My eyes
    follow you, lose you between the trees.

Beside the river, on top of the ancient pine,
    you land and stay still—eyes like blazing orbs, just
    crowned snowy head. Summer is your best time.
     Not like winter when that one-eyed
   mother eagle died foraging in the snow while her
  mate brooded their eggs.

Golden light shines your feathers bronze. A statue.
    A second chance. Not like that father eagle who
      collapsed on the ice, his eyes drifting, then closing
    after eating from a deer shot with a lead bullet.

Within an eyeblink, you're in the water,
   burly talons clutching a big fish,
   wings gliding and slicing
  butterfly strokes through water.

Your nest grows by the year. I hope it lasts.
    Not like the giant nest
     torn by a storm that I found disassembled
  on the ground.

Along the edge of the river, you rise out of
    the crimson ripples.
     Against the headwind, toward the moon,
    you disappear from sight.

A Sheet of Blank Paper

I no longer have a trace of past,
although you are in front of me,
talking about our time together—
The morning fog hung
in the maple forest;
the sunset wove
beside the creek.
You are destined,
to come and leave, naturally,
like the wind that touches
your cheeks, wets my eyes.
Time bleaches the past.
The space between us melts our stories.
No storms in my heart.
I've walked to the far side—
the future waits for new graffiti.

When I'm Walking Backwards

someone asks me,
Do you drive this way, too?

When I'm driving,
the trees speed toward me —
the car and I are a solid union.

My mind, in solidity,
unleashes a thousand wild horses
running to the corners of the twisted world.

When I unearth the darkness
and nurture a grudge against you, my dear,
it is my fault I can't let go.

Island of Cows—São Miguel, Azores

Primavera tries to cross past the wire
to reach the fallen golden nêsperas.
I stroke her head. She nibbles my clothes.
Her Maya-blue irises beam through my heart.
She licks my cheek with her warm, soft
sandpaper tongue. She and her pals graze
ryegrass patch by patch, free & docile
between mountains & sea. Twice a day
the cows give fresh fragrant milk; the cats
& dogs wait for their turn. Below, green
& blue lagoons, still crystal water,
are ringed by fire trees & junipers.
From the volcanic top, heifers—virgin mothers—
line up, watch me leave, deeply lowing.

Ocean Songs

I hear a haunting hymn
   from the surf, primal and
      raw, rolling like your words
   before dying: *Go home,*
stay safe. Oh, dear Popo,
   your heart expands as wide
      as the ocean, as the sun's gilded
   rays. Waves of you pulse
inside me, through every
   cell, ever-renewing—
      through dawn and dusk,
   before and after,
as each dipping sun
   promises a rising one.

Weary from rowing
   and thunder, two
azure boats anchor at the cove
   under layered mosaic
clouds, steadfast.

I'll not linger
   too long
when mountains
   await on the horizon
and sea ripples
   over my feet.

Walking this slick, silver road
    by an outstretched elm,
      beneath a stormy sky, I
    pause at the shore where
an abandoned house looms.
    The drowned may wake, may
      weep. I wander from the dock
    in briny air, step beyond this threshold,
into the hazy light, a candle
    in the window calls me home.

Moonlight Walk

The moon arcs a perfect half-circle. No other stars
flicker except Jupiter in the southern sky and starry
lights from curtained houses; shadows move
across blue-shaded rooms. What story

goes on when the moon is listening?
So do I, the lonely walker, listen
among trees. The continuous drumming
of cicadas, the mooing of a bull-frog,

fill the quiet, warm air. Ardor, I think, yearning.
My body, long ignored, I experience now—
its steps, its sense of moon touch, its sense
of being loved.

A Journey Toward the Ocean

As a wild stream, I thirst for the sea's grandeur and
>   depth. Gravity of longing
>   pulls me forth. Yet I wander
in fresh water scenes,

>   a pond sparkles
>   with purple pickerelweed;

>   a lake surprises me
>   with its bluegills' leap & flicker;

>   a river winds
>   with white water lilies—
a starry purity, a home coming.

Still, the sea remains a haunting distant refrain.
>   Drought descends,
I become less and less—broken by the earth.

In darkness, I curl dormant within a seed.
>   Yet, the sea hums in my bones. I await rain
to split the husk, for light to find me, reborn.

Slowly, I stretch skyward, unfurling
>   green hope, sprouting—
no longer a stream, but a tree.

Steadily I grow, until one day to my own amazement—
>   redbuds blanket all my twigs,
I become my own sea of blooming.

When Dragons Come

Trees can know human intentions. Are we not
as sensitive as trees? But we are afraid.
How to love, if we see through each other
like a penetrating light? How to trust,
when we cannot hide behind our words?
Language or quietness make no difference.
Who thirsts for truth? Who can stomach truth?
Ye Gong Hao Long, the lord who loved Dragons—
had dragons painted on the walls,
carved on pillars and jars.
Yet, when a real dragon came, he ran away.
When dinosaurs we love are reborn
from their own DNA and walk toward us
with huge and heavy steps, will we run?

In the Night

In a pitch-dark night, I wake,
not feeling my body, just my mind.
Thoughts flow by
like a white scarf drifting in darkness.
I will not let my mind escape!
The only thing I can hold onto!
With all my might,
I pull my mind back,
back to my body
on the bed lying flat.

My mind wanders again, trying to leave.
Will death grip me once
I let the mind go?
Is the world a dream? Or
is the world dreaming me?
My curiosity overcomes my fear.
I release my mind.

My mind explodes,
nothing, nothing left, except
the pure vastness.

Cloud Rose

Embellished by stars
Tinged by the last sun-rays
An iridescent pink
Rose in the sky
My eyes pluck it
Hold it in my heart
Knowing it has been or will be
An ocean
A mountain
A horse
Or unseen particles
It doesn't matter

THREE

Under the Autumn High Sky

I keep thinking of my recurring
nightmare—the faceless
dark cloud, this
                hidden suffocation,
not of Gaia that may not save our species,
not of this nation that is doomed,
not my lasting worry about my daughter.
Or maybe I worry about my death, will it be gentle?

Now, the west wind pushes clouds toward the ocean.
Like sip by sip from my tea of ginger, mulberry, and raspberry,
I start dwelling in the afterglow of autumn—
how a tree releases its leaves,
touches the coming winter,
                reaches for the sky,
how the fresh colors' falling
is as beautiful as your passing
when you pulled the tube of your lifeline, my Popo,
                you quietly slipped away.
O, let it pass, my nightmare.

The Missing River

Many times in my dream, a toddler wanders toward
        me, stops and stares, then runs into my arms.
        I hear the summer's chorus,
           singing katydids, and crickets, this is the
   yearning ache that wakes me every time.

This is what I missed when my mother was forced onto
        the labor farm. I was only two, sent to my
grandma in the countryside.

This is what I missed when I was ordered
        not to have a baby while studying
   at university.

This is what I missed when I studied in the states, left
        you, my ten-month-old daughter, home for
        three years. *You were not there for her best
   sunshine smiles*, my mother said.

My lonely journey across the Pacific—
        How many small absences
drop after drop, until I missed the river of you.

Now this late fall, we step on layers of chocolate-
        colored leaves. Rustling echoes through the
        woods. This stream, once dried, is filled from
heavy rains. Branches flow into one river.

Unsung, Five Cinquains

Head high,
Wild turkey struts
Across our frosty street,
Iridescent like a peacock,
Stunning.

Leafless
In wind, in snow,
The stark magnolia tree—
Its buds expand and burst fresh red,
waken.

We bow
To trees for life,
Ignore tiny diatoms,
Every other breath we owe
To them!

The Sun,
Worshiped as God,
Is a monster that burns,
Subdued by the ozone layer,
Disarmed.

Hard-shelled,
Your forthright talk.
You never show your tears.
You help others without fanfare,
Soft inside.

Shuffling Through Old Photographs

You lift me to savor cherry blossoms.
        Our young faces blush.

In another photo, our baby girl laughs, raises the
        stuffed giraffe we bargained for at a yard sale.

In the photo I took in our apartment, a college friend
        plays guitar, at a party that lasted until dusk.

The past has carved our faces, yet our hearts are still in
        spring; and our friend resides in memory now.

Our girl returns after many years of distance, then she
        left us for her own life. Each day, the puppy leads
    our stroll now.

You still hold my hand.
        We don't look back at the dust of scars.

My Popo Talks to the Air

Your finger points to the empty chair in our living room;
you curses someone not there.

Fear clutches my gut, but I won't disturb your lonely
fight. Let the dammed river of your anger burst forth.

This bowl of crucian carp soup you stewed,
holds home remedies for me.

Your Garden of Eden needs this tilling. My silent prayer
hangs heavy in the air as you roll your eyes at the sky.

The moonlight kindles your unhindered shadow, you
soon fall into a forever sleep, your face, an ethereal glow.

The Weight of Time

Dear Popo, I wanted to divide your ashes in half, one half here, the other in our homeland. I've looked at a beautiful high land, yet the wind bites to the bone. And will your soul be restless if not in one place?

Or I could keep you whole here by my side,
through time's passing, through remembering or forgetting, but the call of home I can't deny.

In a handcrafted urn, a sacred marble from India,
You rest, still not claimed by the earth's embrace.

Shall I lay you down in the backyard under the magnolia's bloom?
Will roots hold you steadfast, if we leave?
Will your spirit wander in the night?

Once you longed to cross oceans, to reunite with your love. But there, the burial plot vanishes if not renewed every twenty years.
Who will guard you then?

I hear a whispering in the air,
You were here once.
We, too, shall become "Once" in time.

Autumn Peach

Red-white peaches on the tree
Burning with crunchy sweet saturation
Two wasps buzz, land, and pierce one
Black spots stain the ruddy skin
I pick one and cut to the center
A blushed worm squirms
I slice around
And chew
Ah

The Wind of Emptiness

Its darkness comes & bites,
while the crescent moon
is rising when the sun is still

shining through the blue;
a day the Bloodgood maple
births scarlet propellers.

I let the wind sweep me
to Tai Chi on a hill-yard
surrounded by forest.

The sun lowers
to ridges of trees.
Its tender touch
opens my arms

like a white crane's wings;
I move *Hands Like Clouds*.

Walking the DogBar Breakwater at Gloucester Harbor

Against the blue sky, the red roof,
the East Point Lighthouse
behind us, the sun slips down minute by minute,
on one side the quiet seaport
anchored with boats, on the other,
open ocean—huge waves
strike on granite, endless water splashes our faces &
clothes. We stumble in the wind, pulled to fear's deep
end as if in waves of lost love & wars.
Water flows
from a threatening death roar
through the jetty opening to sunlight
reflections, simmering and rippling.
This narrow path separates, embraces
inside beautiful
& outside perilous.
A young couple with children are fishing,
laughing on the peaceful side, not bothered
by open water. It reminds me of my youth, but
I've seen the stone wall next to
the shore with names of the drowned. I strive to move
my heart along; you take me into your arms.

My New Festivals

The Sad Day Festival pulls me in,
so I can't see the sunrise above the pink clouds,
or hear robins calling each other.

Sadness used to strike at random times on random
days; now, there are new holidays, like Go-Photograph-
Birds, or Poem-Writing-Eve past midnight.

Whenever the chives in the garden grow back after
cutting, or our daughter comes home, there will be
Dumpling-Making-Day.

Among merry days, there will be
Who-Cares-Who-Said-What festivals,
and I delight in my own voice.

Falling Leaves, and Rainy Foggy Days,
are not the Festival of Blue any more,
but Reflection Festivals—the past, the future,
the bridges.

One day, the Festival of Dying will force its way in,
so on Imagine Day, I'll go out, sit beside a tree…

Andrew Jackson's Hermitage in Nashville, Tennessee

I gather three turkey feathers from former cotton
fields—two bronze from the tail, one white-black
from the wing, the pattern interlaced, resembling the
ten-pillared portico.

In the yard stands one Greek temple tomb with two
lovers—a proud general who came daily to talk to his
wife entombed—they rest together now in a garden
of heirloom roses, peonies, and irises.

A few feet away lies Uncle Alfred, the freed slave
who took Jackson's name—
Faithful servant of Andrew Jackson
inscribed on the small tombstone.

I hear Alfred's voice, *How would you like to be a slave?*
as he once asked a tourist visiting the mansion.

The feathers felt heavy. I've seen feathers
glued on Nashvillian guitars. I hear
the new country rap, *What's It Gonna Take.*

Unsettled
—Mid-Autumn Festival

I step outside
into the drizzle. The sky holds
no moon, no stars. It's only a hazy
expanse. I'm simmering
from news, fire, flood, earthquakes, bloodshed…
The five-nut mooncake, a festival staple,
now leaves my body uneasy,
too greasy, too sugary, not quite right,
not like the simple delight from days gone by.
On the sidewalk, a grinning
pumpkin catches my eye.
Beside it, dancing ghosts look like winged
angels. Last night, I watched Whitney Houston's life
unfold, passionate & astonishing. I could hardly
breathe, motionless, as though I was entrapped
in her drug. How her suffering becomes
mine. How many restless hearts dwell
in the ruins, & the moon can't reach their beloved.
Amidst the white ghosts, I hear
crickets serenading. I call my family
across the Pacific. They recovered from Covid
to walk free again.
Tomorrow's moon promises to be flawless.

Fixed

In this twilight of the equinox,
I'm unbalanced.

On the way home in the car
all I hear is my puppy's cry.

Are you still in pain? Are you bemoaning
what has forever been neutered?

I lower the window, see a perfect moon.
The dusky wind sweeps across

your confused face in a plastic cone
like an Elizabethan royal.

I wish you would be quiet, not disturbing
my heart, as if questioning me—

for whose convenience,
whose Cone of Shame?

Horizons

1.

In the soft light of dawn
a dozen croaking ravens line up—
later, an owl
casts his towering shadow,
head twitching and eyes beaming—

I watch them all on the ridge of the rooftop.

2.

Laozi, rode a black ox backwards, bequeathed his book
of Dao; Gautama enlightened under the Bodhi tree;
Jesus prayed in the desert forty days & nights.

What bridged the distance?

We raised Mao's red book, broke statues;
the Beatles started their Magical
Mystery Tour & hippies searched India.

What attuned the fevered hearts?

3.

Walking the fringe where
sanderlings chase & are chased by waves,
light mingles with water in curved patterns.
Gliding sand.
Dancing spindrift.
Touching air.

Right here, right this moment.

Moon Goddess Chang'e Gazing

Yi requested the elixir of immortality from the Queen,
but Chang'e stole it and fled to the moon.

—Han Dynasty, Liu An, circa 139 BC

From the moon, I see candlelight flicker & shadows on
earth below. Shepherd's purse pies & chive dumplings'
steam arise from the rosewood table.
I'll never taste this mortal life again.

I long to hold that box in the glass cabinet filled with
sea treasures, abalone, conch, sand dollar, screw shell
...remnants of days spent with you, Yi—when the moon
split into thousands in the ocean, a dragon root drifted
here & you held me tight under a laurel tree.

Foolish poets gaze up at the crimson moon
and recite dreamy sighs. Do they know how lonely
I am on this desolate moon? Only I watch
the jade rabbit tirelessly pound, mixing
elixirs, hoping one day to return.

I see a woman sober alone in the woods. I would trade
this eternal solidarity for earthly light, even weep like
her in the snow, let icy petals sting my face.

Trace

The moment that could have been remembered, has come and gone, covered in haze.

> —Li Shangyin, Tang Dynasty

When the sun rises,
eight-minute-aged rays alight on my palms.
Our daylilies bloom in response.

The crescent moon looms closer, caresses
my face in seconds with its cool hand.

The last color of the day dwindles.
I step out, look for the Big Dipper,
follow its pointers to Polaris —
my beacon since childhood.

Their centuries-old light arrives,
my timeless sky-companions.

Our memories show up in no time
but will fade one day.
What then sustains us? Will the universe
be our keeper as it remembers stars?

We and the lonely Earth —
the only *Now* we can reach.

A Collection of Shadorma

The Oriole on a Pole

She shrieks at
the beak of a hawk
whose claws crush
her baby
He snaps the prey, flies away
She rushes—too late.

Destined—Indian Summer Flower

One new bud
a rabbit snaps, chews
Two more buds
eaten soon
Equinox comes, three fresh buds
bloom to autumn gold.

Long Winged Hawk

Hovering
high above houses, trees,
laser eyes
scan, steady
wings spiral, drifted circles
—an inner compass.

Diana and the Archer

Along the canal, a silver-haired woman walks
with a service dog. She stops to greet me.

> *My dog is fifteen years old,*
> *still good at reminding me*
> *to stop before I realize I'm exhausted,* she says.
>
> *I was in a wheelchair for fifteen years.*
> Her dog circles around her,
> both in their winter season.

It draws my attention, when I wrestle with my own
fragility, feeling the weight of days, the slow pull of
years. How? Invulnerable in the vulnerable.

> *Now I can stroll longer and longer with his*
> *help.* Her big laughter draws others to look at us.
>
> *I'm always blessed by God, no matter what*
> *you believe. My trust leaves me with no fear.*

Wow. How? Mending the unmendable. A shred of light
touches my brokenness, striving for fresh air.

> She recalls another story. *One time in the*
> *woods, I stood with my bow and arrow aimed*
> *at three men threatening me, and shot over*
> *their heads. They retreated.*

This is Diana—bare-footed, aiming high.
A gust of wind ripples the woman's figure
in the water, colored by a red maple.

No shadow in her voice or on her
face, only a layer of autumn sheen.

Echoes of Birds

—in memory of Li Guozhong, my photography teacher

Clouds move over the tall reeds.
Silky rays pour through the hazy harbor.
Like a Monet's painting. You had stood there,

carrying a long lens, led us birding.
You abruptly crossed time's gate.
When the sun passes the lighthouse

your laughter still echoes in the knee-
deep shore where once we placed our tripods.
Snowy owls return to the island, where

you showed us how to find their
wonder & leave them undisturbed.
I hear you whenever a bird is calling.

Great Meadows in the Autumn

Let's bring my Wounded Love along the dirt road in the
middle of Great Meadows. Let it ache for the yellow
flowers of lotus summer; let it breathe rusty reeds and
sit in a wooden chair, gazing at the water's clouds
where waning lotus float, yellowing and browning.
Let it unwind by bleak wind, cleansed & thirsty
to shed. Nothing wasted—withered leaves, bare
branches & mud, fodder for beaver dams, here, there, in
the marsh. When Wounded Love breaks from tears, let it
trace lotus bent with seeds ready to land, then drawn by
the Great Blue Heron behind stripped stems, moving
stilt by stilt… silent… before the lightning strikes.

FOUR

Fresh Winter

Anxious, isolated,
   boxed in for so long,
     I put yogurt on top
       of wild blueberries
     to start the morning.
   Our dog forces me outside.
I hesitate to walk
   along the snowbank
     piled with the salt-mixed dirty ice.
       He bunny-hops & noses each footprint—
    enchanted as if the first time
   in the pure flickering white—
I open my mouth, touch its coolness.
   Look, the winter buds—
     rhododendron, witch hazel,
       hydrangea & magnolia.
 A fresh song bursts out—
   welcome, wintry chill.
      Welcome, patches of aqua sky.
       My arms open,
    to snow, to frazzle—
   let me savor your melting.
Welcome. Welcome.

Horn Pond Haikus

A Doberman Puppy

cropped, banded ears stand
erect, iconic, three-month-
old is pulled to walk

        A Black Mutt

        jumps to greet our dog
        as fast, spunky, as any,
        with only three legs

A Birch Polypore

on a fallen log
a Razor Strop Fungus carved
with a smiley face

        A Silver Haired-Woman with a Cane Pointing

        They are Mergansers.
        They will leave in early March
        for colder water

You Need to Look Hard

Wooden signs hanging
On bushes, heart-shaped, one says
You are important.

Heavenly Eyes

*In Tianmu's eastern peaks, twin craters rise,
named Heavenly Eyes.
Rocks jut among sparse trees. Wild grasses
scatter the hillside where pigs roam.*
    —my mother labored at the Tianmu
Mountain Ranch, 1959-1962

I am an outcast, a rightist, forced to toil in the Tianmu
Mountain Ranch under Eyes. Beneath a thatched roof,
mud walls separate pig styes from our room storing bean
cakes for swine. I huddle with Nanny and my girl.

Our straw bed lies bare on the hard earth. My one-year-
old quivers as pigs rove and grunt. We inherit no
warmth but pig lice. A doorless passage leads me to the
styes where each night I release pigs to relieve
themselves.

Icy wind whistles, and the pungent air stings. One day,
my past leader appears, and his eyes refuse to meet
mine. The one who stole my diary and accused me of
being a rightist now rears boars below Heavenly.

As sows multiply to hundreds, demands on us mount:
prepare meals, haul water from the river, clean styes,
herd pigs to grasslands. A few villagers are assigned to
help, I share my rations—two meals

of wild veg gruel daily, as managers feast on rice and
wheat. The villagers pilfer sows' bean cakes. One sifts pig

bran, whispers, *Mother's ill,* his eyes plead. I gaze at
sturdy pigs and nod, *Take it!*

Back from a short visit to the village home, Nanny's
bound feet swathed in white, a mourning color. Her eyes
swell. Her husband died of hunger. A villager found and
buried him before she knew.

Where are the Eyes? What is heavenly?

Nanny holds my girl as she scours fields for missed
wheat. She grinds it into flour with small circling strides.
After a wheat porridge reserved solely
for my girl, her eyes sparkle beside pigs
in the shadow of Heavenly Eyes.

Su-Mei from Su-Zhou, China

She can't hold her; tension runs down her spine. The
child was accustomed to being still and alone at the
orphanage. She was abandoned at a farmer's market at
dawn and named after the city where she was found—

a victim of the one-child policy, not a boy.
They bring her home to Boston.

Su-Mei opens a bag of persimmons and eats them like
candies. She follows her father's Tai Chi and topples into
his arms.

Father works late in a chemical lab for more pay,
mother studies physical therapy to help Su-Mei.

You give this girl a better life, I say to my Taichi friend.
She gives us a family and happiness, he says.

One morning, the girl wobbles toward the snow
on the pine branches and calls "Mommy" for the first
time. Father lifts the child and points to
the bald eagle gliding over the clear sky.

Swallow Brand

Sunlight through drapes swirls on the fifty-year-old
sewing machine and your waterfall hair.
With needle threads and scissor snips, your steadfast
hum rhymes with the device's whir and click.

Young people had dressed in hand-me-downs. Each
cherished garment held a braided story beneath your
skilled revision. Labeled a rightist, rendered jobless in a
single stroke— you stitched on, line by line,
pattern by pattern.

In times of rationing, you wove fabric scraps
into shorts and skirts.
You joined a sewing group to craft shoe uppers,
pillowcases, and bags for fifteen yuan monthly—

Pocket money for our beloved Sunday hawthorn
popsicles. We pooled coins to claim a single iced milk
bar—my brother savored half, then gave it to our sister—
but it had melted to the ground.
My sister wept for hours.

Today, you nestle beside the hard-earned heirloom
tailoring fabric to your diminished silhouette.
Your veined hand caresses the engraved name—*Yan Pai*
—*Swallow Brand*—Mother, your fingers fly.

In a Brutal Winter

The war has
no eyes or ears.
No electricity.
No glass windows.
Not even his whisper anymore.
Only fragmented buildings.
Only a candle's flame.
Only empty air to hug.
She knew their goodbye could be
the last one before his fighting
in the front line.
She had prayed, prayed for his return.
Only a child
of her passion
conceived with his preserved sperm
will be out of life and death,
humming for those broken hearted.
Only thunder cracks the grey sky,
but not her will to have,
not just one, as many children
as possible, of his, theirs,
as urgent as when
I was born into this world
right after my parents
survived the forgotten war.
Only luxury of choice
of wanting babies warms a brutal winter.
May those new lives be the green sea
washing away ashes.

In the Great Darkness

After my Popo drifted into eternal slumber, she showed
no signs of pain in her final shape.

She took a solitary journey,
across the last step,

into the great darkness of space—
The earth, the moon, a few shiny jewels,

the gravity that arranges stars,
the love that holds us, living or dead.

She is in the urn,
mosaic green agate.

Waiting, waiting to cross the Pacific
to be with him, my Gonggong, in the motherland

where a dandelion's corona disperses,
suddenly free, free to be an unanchored kite.

I kneel for my father, for yours, his and hers—

So many fathers and mothers,
may my longing keep life going.

The Mystical Blue Rabbit Stamp

This rabbit of 2023 looks so different.
Five-fingered paws hold
a writing brush,
a postcard,
the way a human does.
Is it gathering the names
of dead uncounted before?
Too many fell under a silent foe.
Red moon eyes
burn the mystery
of this winter land.
Is it laughing?
Or sneering?
This harbinger resembles
not the Jade Bunny
flying with Chang'e
to the moon to pound
the mortar for elixir.
A sun-lit scarlet mouth
wide open. Two bare front teeth.
Is it saying, *be watchful?*
Is it saying, *be hopeful?*
It looks like a spirit
of our silenced restless.
The brush resembles a magic wand—
to transmute the darkness, before
the blue exit to the Moon Palace.

New Year

Are you a moment,
or a place?

You come
as you are,
in icy snow.

I remain captive to
the visible 5% of reality I perceive.

I'll not make new resolutions,
that can't be held.
The past is enough to digest.

Adults should be wise.
Children should obey.
Why can't I become who I aspire to be?

Perhaps I do understand,
sub-zero winter
holds the seed of spring.

Sighting a Snowy Owl

Your head swivels. I see so much
in your eyes, big and round,
reflect the setting sun.

You left warming arctic tundra,
migrate to my east
coast town, attracted by
lemmings' booming.

A rarity. A fairy tale.
From your perch on
the dead-wood pole, serene
on the shore's sand dune,
you look down at me.
A spark ignites our silent bond.

And you are not an innocent;
your dignity stops me
with a stern look —
you set the boundary between us.

You will not summer here.
Will you come back?
You remain quiet, like a big-eyed doll

This Body is Not Mine

What if I'm not the only guest
in this transitional house —
bioflora,
trillions of microbiome —
Skin, Mouth, Gut.

Fever claims it,
and I rebel in passion.

I seek to foresee my death
when the body Collective fades.

Yet, of course, we live
and fade at the same time,
like Schrodinger's cat
caught in a quantum mystery—
the fate tied to one radioactive atom,
its random action.

The State has yet to decide—
waiting for the mind's gaze.

Mind Body Duet

*Body: When I was born, your natural soft
radiance bathed my every cell.*

> Mind: I was not aware of you or me
> back then, just air, just play.

> In the verdant years, you brimmed
> rivers of blood, pulsated volcanic energy.

*Yet you drained me ceaselessly,
like drinking from an endless ancestral wellspring.*

> It was your thirst
> that could not be doused.

*Your appetite for sweeter nectar
tempted me into endless toil.*

> You were a silent black box.

*Your dirt clogged my flow,
like fish captured in a net,
pained my neck, arms, and back.*

> I thought you were strong once, an athlete.

*You squeezed the breath from my cells,
propelled me to assail an organ.*

You startled me & my inner quest begins—
Each day, I feel every inch of you & let go
of my clinging.

Lower your pace, listen to my rhythm,
reclaim our shared land.

When the Body Becomes Replaceable Parts

When I first lost my front teeth, I shed
tears. Remember what Confucius said:
the body, hair, and skin are received
from our parents. Dare not damage them.
This is the beginning of filial piety.
Now parts of me have gone: My mouth bone
grafted from others, supported by titanium;
my new teeth ceramic.
                      How else can we be replaced?
A pig valve can keep one's heart beating;
3D printing creates prosthetic limbs; ChatGPT
tries to be our virtual brain.
                            My new teeth chew
well, stir-fried bok choy, baked cod, dumplings.
They, too, join my body and cross the boundary of me.
What is holding the ocean of particles
from the parts, foods, our body, we swim in?

Winter in the Great Meadows

We wander through the meadows for the first time
in the chill, seeing no spring wrens, no summer's lotus
gold, no autumn's lotus pod, no beavers but their lodges.

You say I'm crazy, yet the parking lot is packed, it's not
just me yearning for more even in the winter. The dirt
path submerged in water of foot deep.

You, in your sneakers, pause at the edge. Young lovers
hold hands. The girl removes her shoes, rolls up
her pants and braves the icy puddle.

Don't do that, you are not young,
I caution you. Boots on,
I trudge through the water and the reeds.

On either side of the flooded path,
the meadow gleams through the spiky fresh air,
mirroring the sunlight touching my face.

Lotus tips peep here and there. Geese and swans,
surrounded by tall reeds, glide through
reflections of clouds.

Winter no longer threatens me. A bird, perhaps
a starling, flits before me, alights on a reed.
I heard it has no enemies.

The Great Migration

Dark clouds hang above the muddy river, I hear
hefty wings flapping, and the roll of a rattling
song—a sandhill crane in the air.

Crimson crowns his head like pumped blood.
His extended wings open
toward another crane in front of him.

With big, scaly legs and feet, she steps
forward, barely splashing. She'll stand
in this icy water until dawn.

His ardor, her poised stillness,
resonate within me, kindling
an inner warmth.

My red cap is heart-shaped as hers.
I want to toss weeds with them,
preen, bow, hop & leap into the air

the way they'll couple with each other.
In this moment, I too migrate
beyond the bounds of a reserved self.

Lotus Pond

The golden sun is shining
on the lotus in the forest pond

From the deep mud
purple lotus bloom

A fly touches my lip
I frown, then let it be

A sudden memory of past betrayal
its sting resurfaces, I watch and let it be

I worry about my daughter & the ticking of time
My stomach is tight, but I have to let it be

I hear cries of this world from wars,
from fires, from floods, near and far, my heart is heavy

I look back at the lotus, remind myself
how its beauty rises through the mud

Wakening Between Worlds

Words unpin the veil
of a little girl
I follow her path—
up mountains
down to villages
leaving her baby
her family
her Motherland
sighting virtual neural networks
of herself torn, crushed
lost youth
lost friends
lost wounds
lost words
drawn by woods
drawn by meadow
with swans
with eagles
between the sun and moon
between life and death
between a little country girl
and a woman awakening in the rain—
love, not from outside
but a rooted tree inside
a murmuring thunder
aims my eyes
not a distant horizon
not a shifting target
not a fairyland

not reshaping
the contours of the land
but each moment
pulls her every cell
every word
to stand bare, and as that lake
mirrors ever-changing clouds
leveling water, ice, snow, claiming
Here I am
O my little girl, my little self.

Acknowledgements

Grateful acknowledgment to the following publications in which these poems first appeared, some in different forms:

Art On the Trails Exposure (Elaine and Phillips Beals Preserve, 2022): "Lotus Pond" (as "Where is the Buddha")

The American Journal of Poetry: "Andrew Jackson's Hermitage in Nashville, Tennessee" (as "Andrew Jackson's Hermitage")

Atlanta Review: "Su-Mei from Su-Zhou, China"

The Banyan Review: "Fresh Winter"

Blueline: "A Collection of Shadorma"

Capsule Stories: "Meeting the Great Ancients" (as "Imaging the Great Ancients")

Chautauqua: "Horn Pond in May," "Diana and the Archer" (as "You Need to Be a Good Hunter or a Born Goddess to Get Out of It")

Cider Press Review: "In Our Cypress" (as "On the Cypress in Front of Our House,"), "Shuffling Through Old Photographs"

Cold Mountain Review: "Sighting a Snowy Owl"

The Comstock Review: "A Journey Toward Ocean" (as " Wild Stream,") "Wakening Between Worlds" (as "Arrow from Shadowland")

Crosswinds Poetry Journal: "The Missing River"

Diode Poetry Journal: "In New York City," "What I Once Called Home"

Free State Review: "Island of Cows-São Miguel, Azores," "Echoes of the Eclipse," "Winter in the Great Meadows"

Gravel: "New Year"

HeartWood Literary Magazine: "Echoes of Birds" (as "Kindling")

The Hopper: "Unsung, Five Cinquains"

Jabberwock Review: "Unsettled"

The Lake: "I See No Animals in the Clouds" (as "I See No Animals Anymore")

A Literary Field Guide to Northern Appalachia (University of Georgia Press, 2024): "Between the Sun and Moon"

Longship Press /Nostos: "Two Twelve-Spotted Skimmer Dragonflies"

The Main Street Rag: "Juliets"

The Madison Review: "Moon Goddess Chang'e Gazing"

New Mexico Review: "Horizons" (as "Touching Horizons")
The Midnight Oil: "In the Spring of My Youth" (as "In My Season of Bloom")

MIDLVLMAG : "Heavenly Eyes"

The Nassau Review: "Trace"

Nixes Mate Review: "Firefly"

Nostos: "Under the Autumn High Sky," "Twelve-spotted Skimmer Dragonflies," "Ocean Songs"

Ocean State Review: "Fixed"

PacificReview: "In the Night"

PANK: "Yeye and Me" (as "Philosophy, Art, etc.")

Paper Dragon: "When Dragons Come" (as "Proverb")

Panoplyzine: "The Great Migration" (as "In the Great Migration of Life")

Pedestal: "Swallow Brand"

Poetry Blue River: "Autumn Peach"

Rockvale Review: "Legacy in Loess"

Quartet: "On Marriage"

Rogue Agent: "Mind Body Duet"

Salamander: "To the People, Food is the Sky" (as "The Story of My Sky")

San Pedro River Review: "After the Dragon Boat Festival"

Saranac Review: "The Mystical Blue Rabbit Stamp" (as "The Blue Rabbit Stamp In the Year of Black Rabbit,") "In the Great Darkness" (as "In the Great Darkness, December 2022,") "Walking the DogBar Breakwater at Gloucester Harbor"

Silkworm: "The killdeer"

Slipstream Press: "This Body is Not Mine"

SoFloPoJo: "In a Brutal Winter"

Solstice: "Dichotomy"

Spillway: "Great Meadows in the Autumn"

Spoon River Poetry Review: "The Wind of Emptiness"

Sequestrum: "My Generation" (as "Our Generation,") "My Popo Talks to the Air"

Tampa Review: "Spider Webs"

Turtle Island Quarterly: "Horn Pond Haikus"

Twelve Mile Review: "When the Body Becomes Replaceable Parts," "Cloud Rose"

West Trestle Review: "Moonlight Walk"

Whale Road Review: "Your Breath Mingles with Theirs"
Writers Next Door (Wilmington writing group members, 2018): "My New Festivals," "A Sheet of Blank Paper" as ("I am a Sheet of White Paper,") "Yun Er, Cloud Child, My Betta Fish" (as "Yun Er, Cloud child")

I am grateful to my husband Kaibin who is always the first reader of my poems; to my daughter Yinyin who helps me to reflect deeply on my writing and also provides her editing from time to time; to my father, also a writer, who video-chats with me on art and philosophy; and to my mother who told me the historical stories that I have captured in my poems.

I would like to thank my mentor and teacher, Barbara Helfgott Hyett, who changed my life by guiding me down the beautiful road of poetry; to the PoemWorks community, in particular Wendy Drexler, Margot Wizansky, Sarah Dickenson Snyder, Connemara Wadsworth, Steve Nickman, Cynthia Bargar, Vivian Eyre, Alexis Ivy, Erick Hyett, and Grey Held. Discussion and study within this community have made all of my poems possible and publishable; and to Shana Hill, who has helped me with editing and shepherding my work to the best places for publication.

I am further grateful to the Wilmington Library Poetry Circle, led by Barbara Alevras (later led by me), for her monthly workshop, and to its members: Christine Blaisdell, Maryann Frost, Judith Dettorre, and others who brought me needed perspective.

My gratitude also extends to the support from the Massachusetts Cultural Council for awarding me a 2022 artist fellowship grant in poetry and a 2023 Cultural Sector Recovery Grant. Special gratitude is due to Margot Wizansky, David Rigsbee, Marcela Sulak, and Tennison Black who consulted on and edited my manuscript.

ABOUT THE AUTHOR

Xiaoly Li is a Massachusetts Cultural Council Artist Fellowship Grant (2022) recipient. *Wakening Between Worlds (Serving House Books, 2026) was* short-listed in *2024 Cinnamon Literature Award Adjudication.* Its older version, *Between the Sun and the Moon,* was a finalist in the 2023 *Diode* Editions Book & Chapbook Contests and the *Word Works' 2024 Washington Prize.* Her poetry collection, *Every Single Bird Rising* (FutureCycle Press, 2023), was a Zone 3 Press Book Award finalist. Li's poetry is published in *Crab Orchard Review, Tampa Review, Salamander, Saranac Review, Spillway, Chautauqua, Rhino, Verse Daily,* and elsewhere. She has been nominated for: Best New Poets, five times a Pushcart Prize, four times Best of the Net. She lives in Massachusetts where her photography has been shown and sold in galleries in the Boston area. Her website is www.xiaolyli.art.

www.ingramcontent.com/pod-product-compliance
Lightning Source LLC
Chambersburg PA
CBHW020442090526
44586CB00045B/732